Sew Fun, So Colorful Quilts

FROM ME AND MY SISTER DESIGNS

BARBARA GROVES AND MARY JACOBSON

Sew Fun, So Colorful Quilts

FROM ME AND MY SISTER DESIGNS

Martingale®
& COMPANY

Sew Fun, So Colorful Quilts:
From Me and My Sister Designs
© 2007 by Barbara Groves and Mary Jacobson

That Patchwork Place® is an imprint
of Martingale & Company®.

Martingale & Company
20205 144th Ave. NE
Woodinville, WA 98072-8478 USA
www.martingale-pub.com

Printed in China
12 11 10 09 08 07   8 7 6 5 4 3 2 1

Library of Congress Cataloging-in-Publication Data
Library of Congress Control Number: 2007024478

ISBN: 978-1-56477-770-6

Mission Statement

Dedicated to providing quality products and service to inspire creativity.

Credits

President & CEO ◆ *Tom Wierzbicki*

Publisher ◆ *Jane Hamada*

Editorial Director ◆ *Mary V. Green*

Managing Editor ◆ *Tina Cook*

Developmental Editor ◆ *Karen Costello Soltys*

Technical Editor ◆ *Carol A. Thelen*

Copy Editor ◆ *Sheila Chapman Ryan*

Design Director ◆ *Stan Green*

Assistant Design Director ◆ *Regina Girard*

Illustrator ◆ *Adrienne Smitke*

Cover Designer ◆ *Stan Green*

Text Designer ◆ *Regina Girard & Trina Craig*

Photographer ◆ *Brent Kane*

Contents

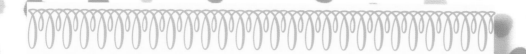

Introduction

WE BELIEVE QUILTS should be used and loved every day. We admire all the work that goes into an antique quilt or a showstopper at the local quilt show, but our quilts will always be fast, fun, and easy!

Bright and scrappy quilts are our favorites, and hunting for fabrics to make them never seems to lose its excitement. We have all our favorite local quilt shops to explore, and also love the adventure of finding wonderful quilt shops as we travel. We are always drawn to the most colorful and whimsical bolts of fabric in the shop.

All of our quilts are pet tested and washer/dryer friendly. Our homes have quilts everywhere—on the walls, covering beds, snuggling on the sofa, and even being used as tablecloths in the kitchen. Sometimes there's even a dog or cat cuddling a quilt on a pile of laundry.

We don't believe in lifelong projects, but we do believe in unfinished projects! Halfway through a project our minds have already wandered to the next quilt. There are so many fabrics to use and patterns to make.

We hope you enjoy making some of the fast, fun, and easy quilts in this book, and that you and your family will cherish them every day.

General Instructions

THESE GENERAL INSTRUCTIONS are to help you along your quilting way, but feel free to use your tried-and-true methods. Enjoy!

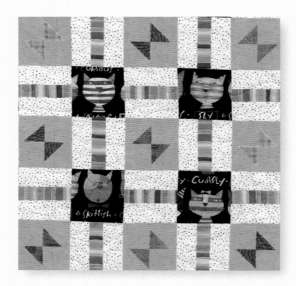

Fabric

All the quilts in this book are made from high-quality 100%-cotton fabrics, and the yardages are based on 40"-wide fabrics. We encourage you to buy extra yardage to allow for shrinkage, trimming selvages, fixing errors—or a slipped ruler.

Prewash, tumble dry, and press the fabrics before using them. We don't like any surprises after we have worked so hard on our quilts, so launder the fabrics the same way you would the completed quilt.

Cutting

All cutting instructions for the projects in this book include a ¼" seam allowance.

Rotary tools have made cutting fast and accurate. Basic tools are a self-healing cutting mat, a rotary cutter, and clear acrylic rulers with easy-to-read measurements.

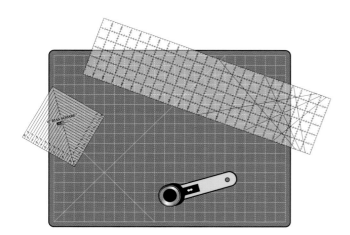

Before cutting, fold and press all fabrics in half, matching the selvages. Place the folded edge closest to you on the cutting mat. When cutting strips, always start with a straightened edge. Align a square ruler along the folded edge of the fabric. Place a longer ruler to the left of the square ruler, just covering the uneven raw edges.

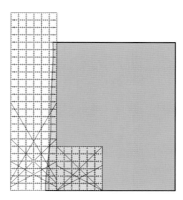

Remove the square ruler and cut along the right edge of the long ruler.

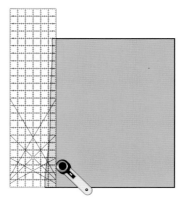

Align the edge of the fabric with the ruler line corresponding to the required width. Cut from the fold to the selvages; stop every few strips and square up the edge of the fabric to avoid a curve in the strips.

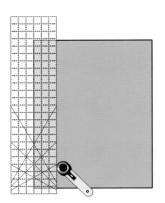

Fussy cutting is when you want to feature the design or picture on a fabric in a specific area of a block. To fussy cut, use a see-through ruler and adjust the ruler to center the picture within the required measurements. This may require the purchase of additional yardage; the amount will depend upon the size and repeat of the picture.

Machine Piecing

It "seams" the most important thing to remember in machine piecing is to maintain an accurate ¼" seam allowance. This will keep all your quilt blocks the desired finished size, and the pieces will fit together perfectly. Set your machine stitch length to 10 to 12 stitches per 1" for a strong seam.

Pressing

The traditional rule in quiltmaking is to press seam allowances to one side, toward the darker color whenever possible. We, however, like to press our seam allowances *open*. This reduces the bulk at seam intersections and gives us more accuracy.

Basic Embroidery

The "Busy Bees" project in this book has an alternative block that uses two basic embroidery stitches. Refer to this section for assistance in creating these whimsical stitches.

Stem Stitch

Cut a workable length of embroidery floss and divide it into three strands. Thread the needle and knot the end of the floss. Bring the needle up at point A. Insert it back into the fabric at point B, about ⅛" away from point A. Holding the floss out of the way, bring the needle back up at point C and pull the floss through so that it lies flat against the fabric. The distances between points A, B, and C should be equal. Pull gently and with equal tension after each stitch.

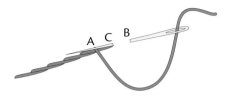

French Knot

Cut a workable length of embroidery floss and divide it into three strands. Thread the needle and knot the end of the floss. Pull the needle from back to front. Wrap the threads around the needle two or three times, and reinsert the needle directly next to the starting point. Use your free hand to hold the thread taut while you pull the needle gently to form a French knot.

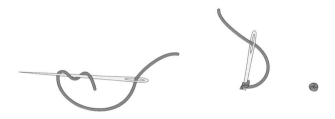

Measuring and Adding Borders

After you have sewn all the blocks and rows together, it's time to add the borders. The instructions for each quilt give you the width and number of border strips to piece together. Measure the quilt from top to bottom through the middle to determine the length of the side borders. Measuring the quilt through the center will provide a more accurate measurement; some stretching and waving of the outer edges may have occurred.

From the pieced border strips, cut the side borders to the measured length. Mark the cen-

ters of the border strips and the quilt top. Pin the borders to the sides of the quilt at the center and ends. Sew the side borders; some easing may be required.

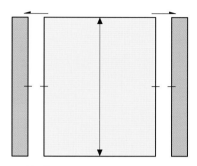

Mark centers. Measure center of quilt, top to bottom.

Measure the quilt from side to side through the middle, including the just-added side borders, to determine the length of the top and bottom borders. From the pieced border strips, cut the top and bottom borders to the measured length. Mark the centers of the border strips and the quilt top. Pin the borders to the top and bottom of the quilt at the center and ends. Sew the top and bottom borders; some easing may be required.

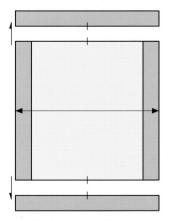

Mark centers. Measure center of quilt, side to side, including borders.

Finishing

Once the quilt top is complete, it's time to make it into a quilt. The backing and batting are layered with the top and all three layers are basted together. Once that is done, the quilting, binding, and any finishing touches are added.

Layering the Quilt

First, assemble the quilt sandwich, which consists of the backing, batting, and quilt top.

We recommend cutting the quilt backing and batting 4" larger than the quilt top on all sides. It might be necessary to piece the backing of your quilt using two or three lengths of fabric. Leftover fabrics and blocks from the quilt top have found their way into our pieced backs and in some cases have given us those few extra inches needed to avoid that second or third length of backing fabric.

Spread the backing, wrong side up, on a flat surface. To keep the backing from moving, use masking tape at the corners and sides to hold it in place. Place the batting over the backing and smooth out any wrinkles. Center the pressed quilt top, right side up, on top of the batting, once again smoothing out any wrinkles.

Basting

Use rustproof safety pins for basting the layers together, starting from the center and working your way to the sides. Place the pins 3" to 4" apart, smoothing as you go. Some quiltmakers prefer to use thread to baste the layers together. If you choose to use thread, use sewing thread and make large basting stitches about 2" to 3" inches apart.

Quilting

Hand or machine quilt as desired. Our desire was that someone else quilt our projects! We love Darlene, our long-arm machine quilter. After the quilting is complete, trim the excess batting and backing even with the quilt top.

Straight-Grain Binding

Binding finishes the raw edges of your quilt. Use straight-grain binding when the edges of the quilt are straight. Each of the quilt projects in this book will give you the required number of binding strips needed as well as the binding method to use. With right sides together, join the ends of the strips on the diagonal to create one long binding strip. Trim the seam allowance to ¼" and press the seam allowance open.

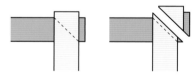

Joining straight-cut strips

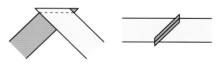

Joining bias strips

1. Fold the binding strip in half lengthwise with wrong sides together and press.

2. Position the binding on the front of the quilt with raw edges aligned. We recommend starting at the center of one of the sides and

leaving a 10" tail (for joining the ends) before beginning the stitching. Using a ¼" seam allowance and a walking foot, sew the binding to the side of the quilt, stopping ¼" from the corner; carefully backstitch 3 or 4 stitches. Clip the thread and remove the quilt from the sewing machine.

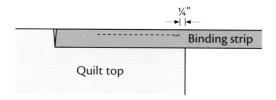

3. Fold the binding strip up, creating a 45° angle.

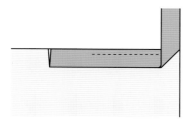

4. Holding the 45° fold in place, bring the binding back down onto itself, and fold it even with the quilt edge. Begin stitching at the folded edge through all layers; carefully backstitch. Continue stitching to the next corner and around the quilt in the same manner.

5. When you have reached a point approximately 10" from the starting point, stop and remove the quilt from the sewing machine.

6. To join the binding ends, fold both strips back along the edge of the quilt so that the folded edges meet an equal distance from both lines of stitching. Press to crease the folds.

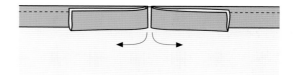

7. Cut both strips 1⅛" from the folds. Open both strips and place the ends at a right angle to each other, right sides together. Join the strips with a diagonal seam as shown. Trim the seam allowance to ¼" and press open.

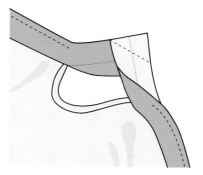

8. Fold the joined strips so that the wrong sides are together again and place the binding flat against the quilt. Finish stitching across the edge of the quilt.

9. Turn the binding over to the back of the quilt and hand stitch using a blind stitch. Make sure to cover the machine stitching. Miter each corner by folding down one side first and then the other.

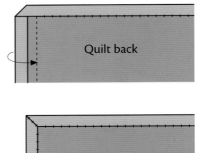

Bias Binding

Bias binding is used to bind the curved edges of a quilt. Cutting the strips along the bias gives the fabric the stretch it needs to lie flat along the curved edge. According to the project directions, the bias binding fabric has been cut into a square. On the wrong side, mark the top and bottom. Cut the square in half on the diagonal.

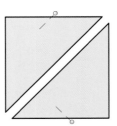

Using a ¼" seam allowance, sew the two triangles, right sides together, along the marked edges. Press the seam allowance open.

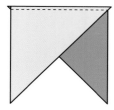

On the wrong side, mark the lines for the 2¼" binding.

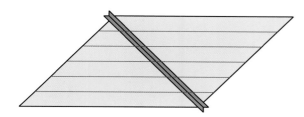

With right sides together, and offsetting the marked lines by one width, sew the fabric into a tube using a ¼" seam allowance.

Press the seam allowance open and cut along the marked lines to make one continuous strip of bias binding.

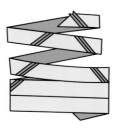

Continue with steps 1–9 of "Straight-Grain Binding" on page 14 to press and attach the binding to the quilt.

Scaredy-Cats

This quick, easy, and fun design
goes together lickety-split.
Three simple blocks are all you need
to complete this quilt just in time
for a catnap. Like dogs?
Chase your tail, turn around
three times, and use your
favorite canine fabrics!

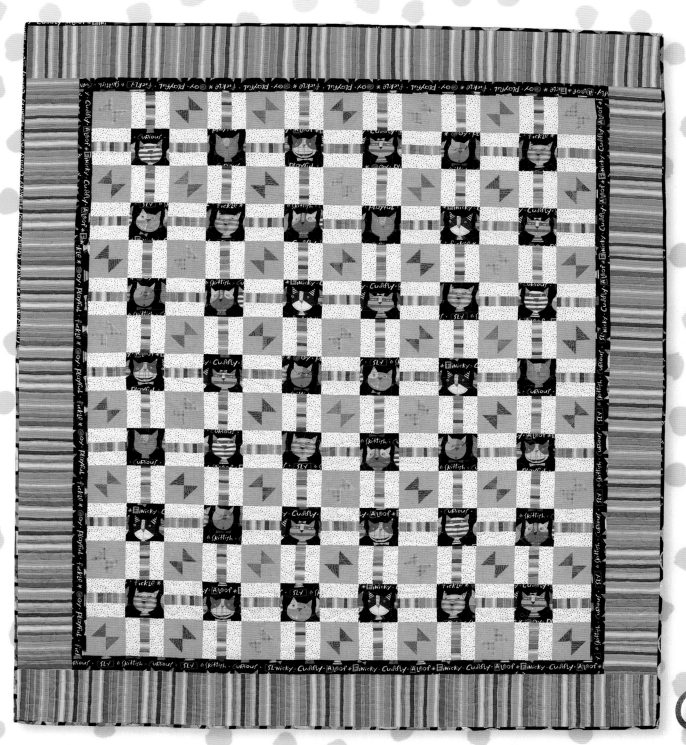

Designed and pieced by Barbara Groves and Mary Jacobson

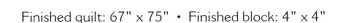

Finished quilt: 67" x 75" • Finished block: 4" x 4"

Materials

All yardages are based on 40"- wide fabric.

2¼ yards of orange stripe for Rail blocks and
    second border

1¾ yards of dot print for Rail blocks

1¼ yards of orange fabric for Bow Tie blocks

1 yard of cat print for Cat blocks (additional
    yardage may be needed for fussy cutting)

1 fat quarter *each* of pink, purple, blue, and green
    fabrics for Bow Tie blocks

1 yard of fabric for first border and binding

5 yards of fabric for backing

75" x 83" piece of batting

Cutting

FROM THE DOT PRINT, CUT:

26 strips, 2" x 40"

FROM THE ORANGE STRIPE, CUT:

13 strips, 1½" x 40"

7 strips, 6¼" x 40"

FROM THE FAT QUARTERS, CUT:

26 pink squares, 2" x 2"

26 purple squares, 2" x 2"

28 blue squares, 2" x 2"

32 green squares, 2" x 2"

FROM THE ORANGE FABRIC, CUT:

14 strips, 2½" x 40"; crosscut into 224 squares,
    2½" x 2½"

FROM THE CAT PRINT, CUT:

6 strips, 4½" x 40"; crosscut into 42 squares,
4½" x 4½"

**FROM THE FIRST-BORDER AND BINDING
FABRIC, CUT:**

6 strips, 2" x 40"

8 strips, 2¼" x 40"

Making the Blocks

1. Sew a 2" x 40" dot strip to each side of the
1½" x 40" orange stripe strips. Press the seam
allowances open.

2. Crosscut the strip sets into 4½" segments to
make 97 Rail blocks.

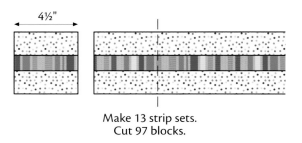

Make 13 strip sets.
Cut 97 blocks.

3. Draw a diagonal line on the wrong side of
each 2" pink, purple, blue, and green square.

4. With right sides together, place a 2" square
on the corner of a 2½" orange square as
shown. Stitch on the marked line. Trim the
seam allowance to ¼". Flip and press the
seam allowances open. Repeat with the other
2" squares.

5. Keeping like colors together, arrange and sew
the Bow Tie blocks as shown.

Make 56.

Assembling the Quilt

1. Alternating blocks, arrange and sew seven Rail and six Cat blocks into a row as shown. Make seven rows.

Make 7.

2. Alternating blocks, arrange and sew seven Bow Tie and six Rail blocks into a row as shown. Tilt the Bow Tie blocks in different directions to create fun. Make eight rows.

Make 8.

3. Sew the rows together, starting and ending with Bow-Tie block rows and alternating with Cat-block rows. The quilt should now measure 52½" x 60½".

Adding the Borders

1. Piece the six 2" x 40" first-border strips end to end. Refer to "Measuring and Adding Borders" on page 13 to cut and attach the first border. The quilt should now measure 55½" x 63½".

2. Piece the seven 6¼" x 40" orange stripe strips end to end; cut and attach the second border.

Finishing

Refer to "Finishing" on page 14 to layer, baste, quilt, and add the binding.

Quilt plan

Piranha

Gather your blue, green, and yellow fabrics
and take a quilting trip down the Amazon.
Imagine half-square triangles as razor-
sharp teeth lurking just below the water's
surface. This simple Rail Fence block set
on point is less treacherous than you think.
Please keep your hands and feet inside
the boat at all times!

Designed and pieced by Mary Jacobson and Barbara Groves

Finished quilt: 84" x 84" • Finished block: 9"x 9"

Materials

All yardages are based on 40"- wide fabric.

½ yard *each* of 10 light blue fabrics for blocks and second border

⅜ yard *each* of 11 dark blue fabrics for blocks and second border

7 fat quarters of green fabric for blocks

5 fat quarters of light blue fabric for setting and corner triangles

5 fat quarters of dark blue fabric for setting and corner triangles

1 yard of yellow fabric for blocks

⅜ yard of green fabric for first border

¾ yard of green fabric for binding

7¾ yards of fabric for backing

92" x 92" piece of batting

Cutting

FROM THE YELLOW FABRIC, CUT:

7 strips, 3⅞" x 40"; crosscut into 63 squares, 3⅞" x 3⅞"

FROM *EACH* GREEN FAT QUARTER, CUT:

9 squares, 3⅞" x 3⅞" (63 total)

FROM *EACH* LIGHT BLUE FABRIC FOR BLOCKS AND SECOND BORDER, CUT:

6 strips, 2" x 40" (60 total); crosscut into 202 rectangles, 2" x 9½"

FROM *EACH* DARK BLUE FABRIC FOR BLOCKS AND SECOND BORDER, CUT:

3 strips, 3½" x 40" (33 total); crosscut into 101 rectangles, 3½" x 9½"

FROM *EACH* LIGHT BLUE AND DARK BLUE FAT QUARTER, CUT:

1 square, 10½" x 10½" (10 total); cut each square once diagonally to yield 20 triangles

FROM THE GREEN FABRIC FOR FIRST BORDER, CUT:

7 strips, 1½" x 40"

FROM THE GREEN FABRIC FOR BINDING, CUT:

9 strips, 2¼" x 40"

Making the Blocks

1. Draw a diagonal line on the wrong side of each 3⅞" yellow square.

2. With right sides together, layer one yellow and one green 3⅞" square together. Stitch ¼" away from each side of the drawn line. Cut on the drawn line and press the seam allowances open. The half-square triangles should measure 3½" square.

3. Make 126 half-square triangles. You will only use 123 of these, so choose your favorites!

4. Arrange and sew half-square triangles, light blue rectangles, and dark blue rectangles into blocks A and B as shown. Make 25 of block A and 16 of block B.

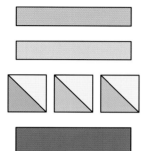

Block A.
Make 25.

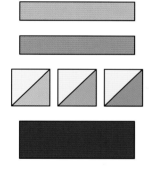

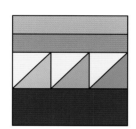

Block B.
Make 16.

Assembling the Quilt

1. Referring to the assembly diagram at right, arrange and sew the blocks and the dark and light blue setting triangles into rows. Attach the corner triangles last. The setting and corner triangles have been cut larger than needed.

2. Trim the quilt ¼" beyond the block points. The quilt should now measure 64¼" square.

Quilt assembly

Adding the Borders

1. Piece the 1½" x 40" green border strips end to end. Refer to "Measuring and Adding Borders" on page 13 to cut and attach the green border. The quilt should now measure 66¼" square.

2. Piece 60 dark blue rectangles together, side by side.

3. Piece 120 light blue rectangles together, side by side.

4. Measure the quilt from top to bottom through the middle to determine the length of the side borders.

5. From the dark blue border strip, cut the left side border to the measured length and attach it to the left side of the quilt (the light-setting-triangle side).

6. From the light blue border strip, cut the right side border to the measured length and attach it to the right side of the quilt (the dark-setting-triangle side).

7. Measure the quilt from side to side through the middle, including the just-added borders, to determine the length of the top and bottom borders.

8. From the light blue border strip, cut the top border to the measured length and attach it to the top of the quilt (the dark-setting-triangle side).

9. From the dark blue border strip, cut the bottom border to the measured length and attach it to the bottom of the quilt (the light-setting-triangle side).

Finishing
Refer to "Finishing" on page 14 to layer, baste, quilt, and add the binding.

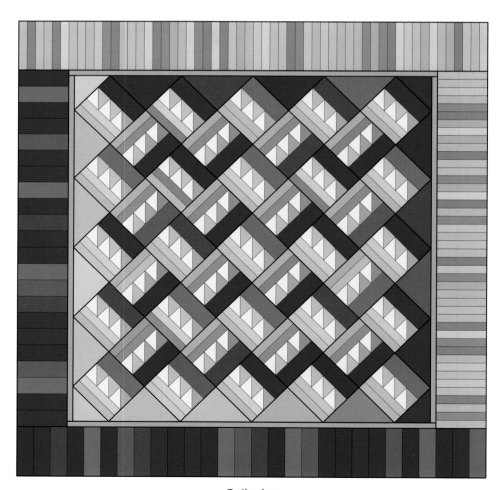

Quilt plan

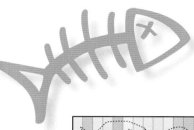

Quilting suggestion

Feed Me, Audrey

Plant fabric flowers in these easy-to-make whimsical flowerpots! Watch them bloom into a colorful garden of fun. Show your creativity using your favorite buttons to form stems and to embellish flowers and leaves. This small quilt is sure to bring a bouquet of color to any room.

Designed and pieced by Mary Jacobson and Barbara Groves

Finished quilt: 52" x 52"

Materials

All yardages are based on 40"- wide fabric unless otherwise noted.

2⅛" yards of white print for blocks, sashing, and first border

1 yard of dark green fabric for second border

¼ yard of purple stripe for flowerpots

4" x 4" scrap *each* of 34 different green fabrics for first border

5" x 5" scrap *each* of 13 different green fabrics for leaves

8" x 10" scrap *each* of light, medium, and dark yellow fabrics for flowers and first border

8" x 8" scrap *each* of light, medium, and dark turquoise fabrics for flowers and first border

8" x 8" scrap *each* of light, medium, and dark orange fabrics for flowers and first border

8" x 8" scrap *each* of light, medium, and dark pink fabrics for flowers and first border

4" x 4" scrap *each* of light, medium, and dark purple fabrics for flower

5" x 15" scrap of dark green fabric for leaf tips

9" x 13" scrap of dark green fabric for flower-base leaves

8" x 9" scrap of purple dot print for flowerpot bands

½ yard of dark green fabric for binding

3½ yards of fabric for backing

56" x 56" piece of batting

Approximately 68 buttons in assorted colors, shapes, and sizes

Sewing needle and sewing thread for buttons

Cutting

Flowerpots

FROM THE PURPLE DOT FOR FLOWERPOT BANDS, CUT:

5 rectangles, 1½" x 6½"

FROM THE PURPLE STRIPE FOR FLOWERPOTS, CUT:

1 strip, 1½" x 40"; crosscut into 5 rectangles, 1½" x 6½"

1 strip, 4½" x 40"; crosscut into 5 rectangles, 4½" x 6½"

FROM THE WHITE PRINT, CUT:

2 strips, 2½" x 40"; crosscut into 10 rectangles, 2½" x 6½"

Flowers

FROM THE WHITE PRINT, CUT:

1 strip, 2½" x 40"; crosscut into 14 squares, 2½" x 2½"

1 strip, 3¼" x 40"; crosscut into 10 squares, 3¼" x 3¼"

3 strips, 4" x 40"; crosscut into 23 squares, 4" x 4". Cut each square once diagonally to yield 46 triangles.

FROM *EACH* LIGHT TURQUOISE, ORANGE, AND PINK FABRIC, CUT:

2 squares, 3¼" x 3¼" (6 total)

FROM *EACH* DARK TURQUOISE, ORANGE, AND PINK FABRIC, CUT:

4 squares, 2⅞" x 2⅞" (12 total)

FROM *EACH* MEDIUM TURQUOISE, ORANGE, AND PINK FABRIC, CUT:

3 squares, 2½" x 2½" (9 total)

FROM THE LIGHT YELLOW FABRIC, CUT:

3 squares, 3¼" x 3¼"

FROM THE DARK YELLOW FABRIC, CUT:

5 squares, 2⅞" x 2⅞"

FROM THE MEDIUM YELLOW FABRIC, CUT:

4 squares, 2½" x 2½"

FROM THE LIGHT PURPLE FABRIC, CUT:

1 square, 3¼" x 3¼"

FROM THE DARK PURPLE FABRIC, CUT:

1 square, 2⅞" x 2⅞"

FROM THE MEDIUM PURPLE FABRIC, CUT:

1 square, 2½" x 2½"

FROM THE DARK GREEN FABRIC FOR FLOWER-BASE LEAVES, CUT:

5 squares, 4" x 4"; cut each square once
    diagonally to yield 10 triangles

Leaves

FROM THE DARK GREEN FABRIC FOR LEAF TIPS, CUT:

13 squares, 2" x 2"

FROM THE WHITE PRINT, CUT:

1 strip, 2" x 40"; crosscut into 13 squares, 2" x 2"
2 strips, 3" x 40"; crosscut into 13 rectangles,
    3" x 4"

FROM THE 13 DIFFERENT GREEN FABRICS FOR LEAVES, CUT:

1 square, 4" x 4" (13 total)

Sashing and Quilt Center

FROM THE WHITE PRINT, CUT:

1 strip, 6½" x 40"; crosscut into:
    1 rectangle, 4" x 6½"
    1 rectangle, 5" x 6½"
    1 rectangle, 2" x 6½"
    1 rectangle, 4" x 6½"
6 strips, 1½" x 40"; crosscut into 6 rectangles,
    1½" x 35"
1 strip, 2" x 40"; cut into 1 rectangle, 2" x 36½"

Borders and Binding

FROM THE WHITE PRINT, CUT:

3 strips, 2⅞" x 40"; crosscut into 34 squares,
    2⅞" x 2⅞"

FROM THE 34 DIFFERENT GREEN FABRICS FOR FIRST BORDER, CUT:

34 squares, 2⅞" x 2⅞"

FROM THE DARK GREEN FABRIC FOR SECOND BORDER, CUT:

5 strips, 6¼" x 40"

FROM DARK GREEN FABRIC FOR BINDING, CUT:

6 strips, 2¼" x 40"

Making the Units

Four different units are used to make the interior of this quilt: flowerpots, flowers, flowers with leaves, and leaves. The units are pieced into vertical rows to form the interior of the quilt top.

Flowerpots

1. Sew a 1½" x 6½" purple dot rectangle to the top of a 4½" x 6½" purple stripe rectangle.

2. Measure in ¼" from each side at the top of the pot segment and make a pencil mark.

3. Measure in 1¼" from each side at the bottom of the pot segment and make a pencil mark.

4. Draw a line between the top and bottom mark on each side. Cut on the drawn line.

5. With right sides together, sew a 2½" x 6½" white print rectangle to each side of the previous segment. Flip and press the seam allowances open.

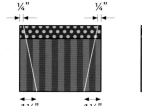

6. With right sides together, align the side of a 1½" x 6½" purple stripe rectangle along the top edge of the purple dot rectangle. Sew a ¼" seam across the entire unit. Flip and press the seam allowances open.

7. Trim the unit to 6½" x 6½". Make five.

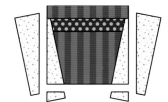

Make 5.

Flowers

1. Draw a diagonal line on the wrong side of two 3¼" white print squares.

2. With right sides together, layer a marked 3¼" white print square and a 3¼" light turquoise square together. Stitch ¼" away from each side of drawn line. Cut apart on the drawn line and press the seam allowance open. The half-square triangles should measure 2⅞" square. Repeat with another set of squares to make four total half-square triangles.

Make 4.

3. Draw a diagonal line on the wrong side of the four 2⅞" light turquoise half-square triangles. The drawn line must bisect the seam line.

4. With right sides together, layer a marked 2⅞" light turquoise half-square triangle and a 2⅞" dark turquoise square together. Stitch ¼" away from each side of drawn line. Cut apart on the drawn line and press the seam allowances open. The flower petals should measure 2½" square.

5. Repeat with the other sets of squares to make eight flower petals. Set two aside to be used in the first border.

Make 8.

6. Arrange and sew two flower petals, a 2½" white print square, and a 2½" medium turquoise square into flowers. Make three turquoise flowers.

Make 3.

7. Repeat steps 1–6 using light and dark orange and light and dark pink fabrics. Make three orange and three pink flowers.

Make 3.   Make 3.

8. For the light and dark yellows, repeat steps 1 and 2 using three background squares to make six half-square triangles. Repeat steps 3–5 to make 10 flower petals; set two aside to be used in the first border. Repeat step 6 to make four yellow flowers.

Make 4.

9. For the light and dark purple, repeat steps 1 and 2 using one background square to make two half-square triangles. Repeat steps 3–5 to make two flower petals. Repeat step 6 to make one purple flower.

Make 1.

10. Using two each of the turquoise, orange, and pink flowers and three of the yellow flowers, arrange and sew a flower and four white print triangles into units as shown.

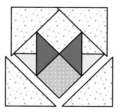 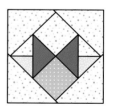

Make 2 each of turquoise, orange, and pink.
Make 3 yellow.

Flowers with Leaves

Using the purple flower and the remaining flowers of each color, arrange and sew a flower, two white print triangles, and two dark green flower-base leaf triangles into a flower-with-leaf unit as shown.

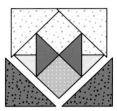 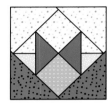

Make 1 each of turquoise, orange, pink, and yellow.

Leaves

1. Draw a diagonal line on the wrong side of the 13 dark green leaf-tip 2" squares and the 13 white print 2" squares.

2. With right sides together, position a green and white print square on opposite corners of a 4" leaf square. Stitch on the marked lines. Trim the seam allowances to ¼". Flip and press the seam allowances open.

Make 13.

3. Sew a 3" x 4" white print rectangle to the side of each leaf unit to create two different leaf shapes as shown. Make 13.

  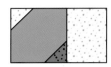

Make 6.

Make 7.

Assembling the Quilt

Arrange and sew the units and white print rectangles into vertical rows as shown in the assembly diagram on page 35.

Sashing

1. Sew 1½" x 35" sashing rectangles between the vertical flower rows as shown in the assembly diagram. Add one to each end.

2. Sew the 2" x 36½" bottom sashing rectangle to quilt center.

First Border

1. Draw a diagonal line on the wrong side of the 34 white print 2⅞" squares.

2. With right sides together, layer a marked 2⅞" white print square and a 2⅞" green border square together. Stitch ¼" away from each side of drawn line. Cut apart on the marked line and press the seam allowances open. The half-square triangles should measure 2½" square. Make 68. Set aside four to be used as corners.

3. Sew eight half-square triangles into border segment A and eight half-square triangles into border segment B as shown. Make four of each.

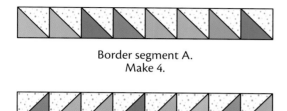

Border segment A.
Make 4.

Border segment B.
Make 4.

4. Sew the two turquoise flower petal units into a flower bud as shown.

Make 1.

5. Repeat for the orange, pink, and yellow flower bud units.

6. Arrange and sew a border segment A, a border segment B, and a flower bud into a row as shown.

Make 1 of each turquoise, orange, pink, and yellow.

7. Attach the yellow and orange border rows to the sides of the quilt.

8. Sew a half-square triangle to each end of the remaining turquoise and pink border rows as shown.

9. Attach the border rows to the top and bottom of the quilt.

Second Border

Sew the five 6¼" x 40" second border strips end to end. Refer to "Measuring and Adding Borders" on page 13 to cut and attach the second border.

4 x 6½"   5 x 6½"   2 x 6½"   4 x 6½"

Quilt assembly

Quilt plan

Finishing

Refer to "Finishing" on page 14 to layer, baste, quilt, and add the binding. Refer to the photo on page 29 for the placement of the buttons. Using the sewing needle and thread, stitch the buttons securely in place.

Busy Bees

Catch a buzz making this sweet-as-honey quilt! Stitch a path though this fun Snowball and Shoofly design. Our quilt was made using a whimsical novelty fabric that features chubby bees, but we've also provided directions for embroidering the blocks with the bee pattern on page 41.

Designed and pieced by Barbara Groves and Mary Jacobson

Finished quilt: 74" x 74" • Finished block: 8" x 8"

Materials

All yardages are based on 40"- wide fabric

2½ yards of pink bee print for block centers (or white fabric if embroidering the bees; see "Optional Embroidery Materials" below)

10 fat quarters of red fabric for blocks and sashing

1¾ yards of pink print for border

1⅓ yards of black dot for sashing

1 yard of pink print for bias binding

4¾ yards of fabric for backing

82" x 82" piece of batting

Optional Embroidery Materials

2½ yards of white fabric for block centers (instead of the pink bee print)

Embroidery needle

One skein *each* of the following colors of DMC embroidery floss: 333, 340, 413, 704, 741, 743, 905, 943, 956, 964, 3708, and 3824

Cutting

FROM EACH FAT QUARTER OF RED FABRIC, CUT:

15 squares, 3½" x 3½" (150 total; you will have 6 extra)

5 squares, 2" x 2" (50 total; you will have 1 extra)

FROM THE PINK BEE PRINT, CUT:

9 strips, 8½" x 40"; crosscut into 36 squares, 8½" x 8½"

FROM THE BLACK DOT, CUT:

5 strips, 8½" x 40"; crosscut into 84 rectangles, 2" x 8½"

FROM THE PINK PRINT FOR BORDER, CUT:

7 strips, 8" x 40"

FROM THE PINK PRINT FOR BIAS BINDING, CUT:

1 square, 30" x 30"

Making the Blocks

1. Draw a diagonal line on the wrong side of each 3½" red square.

2. With right sides together and using four matching red fabrics, place a 3½" red square on each corner of an 8½" pink bee print square. Stitch on the drawn lines. Trim the seam allowances to ¼". Flip and press the seam allowances open.

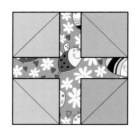
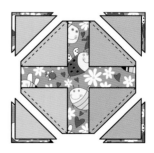

3. Optional: If desired, use the bee-motif pattern on page 41 to embroider on any or all of the blocks. Refer to "Basic Embroidery" on page 12 for embroidery instructions. Use the stem stitch to outline the bees and flowers and a French knot to embellish the design.

Assembling the Quilt

1. Starting and ending with a 2" red square, arrange seven red squares and six 2" x 8½" black dot sashing rectangles into a row as shown. Make seven.

Make 7.

2. Starting and ending with a 2" x 8½" black dot sashing rectangle, alternate seven sashing rectangles and six 8½" blocks into a row as shown. Make six.

Make 6.

3. Arrange and sew the sashing and block rows together as shown in the quilt plan at right. The quilt should now measure 59" square.

Adding the Border

Piece the seven 8" x 40" pink border strips end to end. Refer to "Measuring and Adding Borders" on page 13 to cut and attach the border.

Finishing

Refer to "Finishing" on page 14 to layer, baste, and quilt the quilt top, but do not trim the edges. Instead, use the scallop-edge template on page 40 as a guide to trim the border. Refer to "Bias Binding" on page 16 to prepare and attach the bias binding.

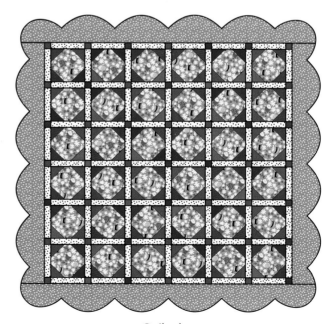

Quilt plan

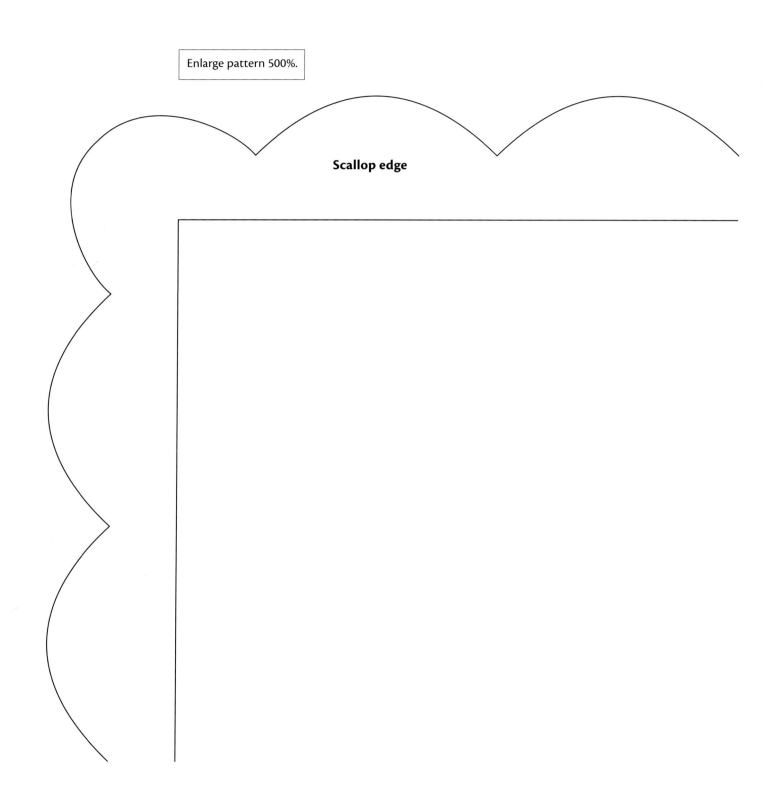

Enlarge pattern 500%.

Scallop edge

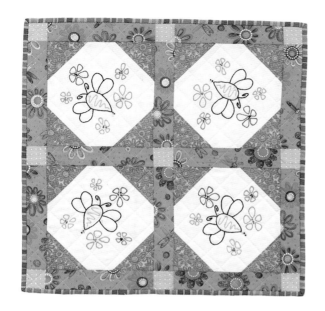

A smaller version of the quilt, made in bright springtime colors and without the scalloped border, features the embroidered bees.

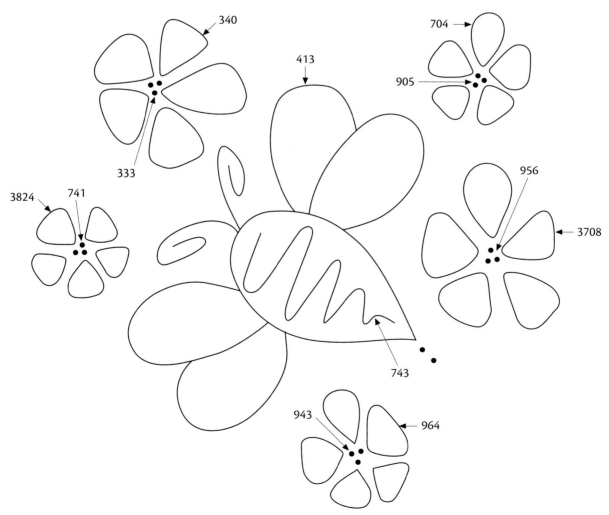

Embroidery pattern and DMC floss guide

Along Came a Spider

Along came a spider and

sat down beside her . . . but don't let

this quilt scare you away! Strip sets

and half-square triangles make this

quilt go together in no time at all.

Collecting fat quarters for this scrappy

quilt is more fun than eating curds . . .

and by the whey, what is a curd?

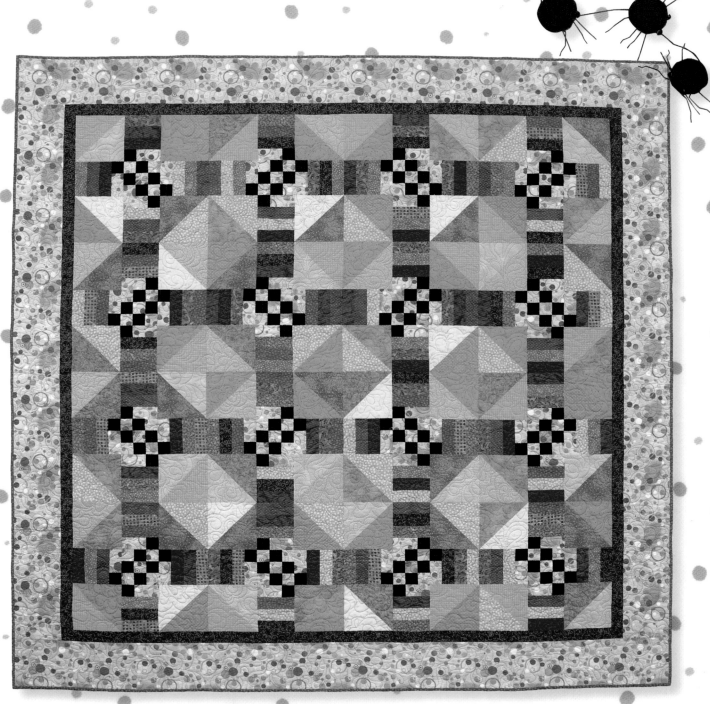

Designed and pieced by Mary Jacobson and Barbara Groves

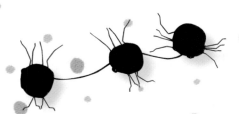

Finished quilt: 84" x 84" • Finished block: 16½" x 16½"

Materials

All yardages are based on 40"- wide fabric

16 fat quarters of turquoise fabrics for blocks
(use scraps for more variety)

2½ yards of purple-and-turquoise print for blocks
and second border

8 fat quarters of purple fabrics for blocks
(use scraps for more variety)

⅝ yard of black fabric for blocks

⅝ yard of dark purple fabric for first border

¾ yard of medium purple fabric for binding

7¾ yards of fabric for backing

92" x 92" piece of batting

Cutting

FROM THE PURPLE-AND-TURQUOISE PRINT, CUT:

5 strips, 2" x 40"
4 strips, 3½" x 40"
8 strips, 6¾" x 40"

FROM THE BLACK FABRIC, CUT:

8 strips, 2" x 40"

FROM EACH FAT QUARTER OF PURPLE FABRIC, CUT:

24 rectangles, 2" x 5" (192 total)

FROM EACH FAT QUARTER OF TURQUOISE FABRIC, CUT:

4 squares, 6⅞" x 6⅞" (64 total)

FROM THE DARK PURPLE FABRIC, CUT:

8 strips, 2" x 40"

FROM THE MEDIUM PURPLE FABRIC, CUT:

9 strips, 2¼" x 40"

Making the Blocks

Each block consists of a center Nine Patch; strip-pieced squares for the top, bottom, and sides; and half-square triangles for the corners.

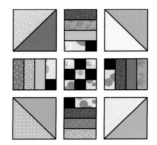 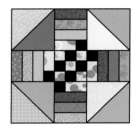

Nine Patches

1. To make strip set A, sew a 2" x 40" purple-and-turquoise print strip to each side of a 2" x 40" black strip. Make two.

2. Crosscut the strip sets into 32 segments, 2" each.

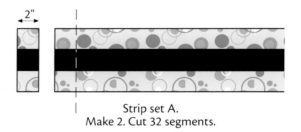

Strip set A.
Make 2. Cut 32 segments.

3. To make strip set B, sew a 2" x 40" black strip to each side of a 2" x 40" purple-and-turquoise print strip. Make one.

4. Crosscut the strip set into 16 segments, 2" each.

Strip set B.
Make 1. Cut 16 segments.

5. Arrange and sew two strip-set A segments and one strip-set B segment into a Nine Patch block as shown. Make 16.

Nine Patch block.
Make 16.

Rectangles

1. To make strip-set C, sew a 2" x 40" black strip to the top of a 3½" x 40" purple-and-turquoise strip. Make four.

2. Crosscut the strip sets into 64 segments, 2" each.

Strip set C.
Make 4. Cut 64 segments.

3. Arrange and sew 2" x 5" purple rectangles and strip-set C segments into two units as shown. Make 32 of each unit.

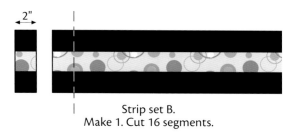

Make 32.   Make 32.

Half-Square Triangles

1. Draw a diagonal line on the wrong side of 32 turquoise 6⅞" squares.

2. With right sides together, layer a marked and unmarked turquoise 6⅞" square. Stitch ¼" away from each side of drawn line. Cut apart on the drawn line and press the seam allowances open. The half-square triangles should measure 6½" square. Make 64.

Make 64.

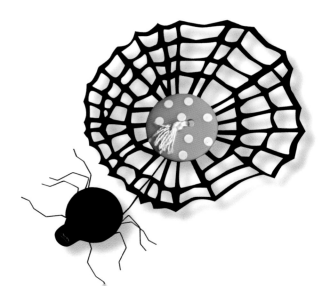

Assembling the Blocks

Arrange and sew the units into 16 blocks as shown in the block diagram on page 44. Blocks should measure 17" square.

Assembling the Quilt

Arrange the blocks as shown in the quilt plan below. Note the alternate rotation of the block centers. Sew four rows of four blocks each. Sew the rows together as shown. The quilt should now measure 68½" square.

Adding the Borders

1. Piece the eight 2" x 40" dark strips end to end. Refer to "Measuring and Adding Borders" on page 13 to cut and attach the first border.

2. Piece the eight 6¾" x 40" purple-and-turquoise strips end to end. Measure, cut, and attach the second border.

Finishing

Refer to "Finishing" on page 14 to layer, baste, quilt, and add the binding.

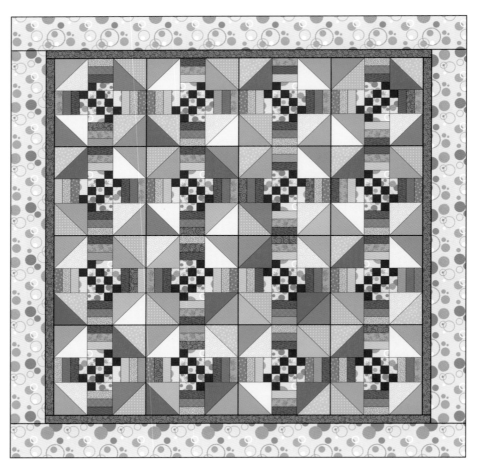

Quilt plan

Quilting suggestion

String Beans

Calling all colors!
Collect "string beans," or strips, from
your favorite fabrics to create this
cheerful cuddle-up quilt. Sewing string
beans onto a foundation square will
keep your bias under control. It's a
good way to get your veggies!

Designed and pieced by Mary Jacobson and Barbara Groves

Finished quilt: 71" x 75" • Finished block: 10" x 10"

Materials

All yardages are based on 40"- wide fabric

36 assorted fat quarters for blocks

4 yards of white muslin for block foundations

⅝ yard of pink print for border

⅝ yard of green print for border

½ yard of yellow print for border

½ yard of orange print for border

¾ yard of stripe for binding

5 yards of fabric for backing

79" x 83" piece of batting

Cutting

FROM EACH FAT QUARTER, CUT:

2 strips, 2¾" x 20" (72 total)

2 strips, 2¼" x 20" (72 total)

2 strips, 1¾" x 20" (72 total)

2 strips, 1¼" x 20" (72 total)

FROM THE WHITE MUSLIN, CUT:

12 strips, 11" x 40"; crosscut into 36 squares,
11" x 11"

FROM EACH YELLOW AND ORANGE PRINT, CUT:

2 strips, 5¾" x 40" (4 total)

FROM EACH PINK AND GREEN PRINT, CUT:

2 strips, 7¾" x 40" (4 total)

FROM THE STRIPE, CUT:

8 strips, 2¼" x 40"

Making the Blocks

1. Place a fat-quarter strip of any width *right side up* diagonally across the center of an 11" muslin foundation square.

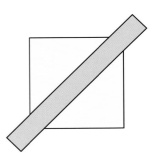

2. With *right sides together,* place another fat-quarter strip on top of the center strip; align the side edges. Make sure your strips always extend beyond the muslin foundation.

3. Stitch a ¼" seam along the edge through all layers. Flip and press toward the corner.

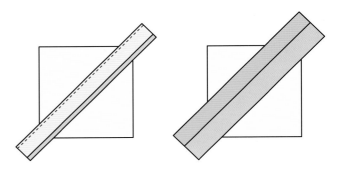

4. Continue adding strips to each side of the center strip until the muslin foundation is completely covered. Be creative; use different widths and colors so that no two blocks are the same!

5. From the back side, trim the blocks (including both the muslin foundation and the top fabrics) to measure 10½" square. The muslin

foundation helps control the bias edges. The trimmed-off pieces can be used in other projects. Make 36.

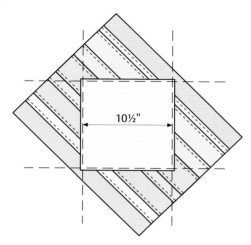

10½"

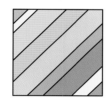

Make 36.

Assembling the Quilt

Rotate the blocks as shown in the quilt plan at right. Sew six rows of six blocks each. The quilt should now measure 60½" square.

Side Borders

1. Piece the two 5¾" x 40" yellow border strips end to end and piece the two 5¾" x 40" orange border strips end to end. Press the seam allowances open. The yellow strip will be attached to one side of the quilt top and the orange strip will be attached to the opposite side.

2. Measure the quilt from top to bottom through the middle to determine the length of the side borders.

3. From *each* pieced strip, cut a side border to the measured length; attach to opposite sides of the quilt.

Top and Bottom Borders

1. Piece the two 7¾" x 40" pink border strips end to end and piece the two 7¾" x 40" green border strips end to end. The pink strip will be attached to the top and the green strip will be attached to the bottom.

2. Measure the quilt from side to side through the middle including the side borders to determine the length of the top and bottom borders.

3. From *each* pieced strip, cut a border to the measured length; attach the pink border to the top of the quilt and the green border to the bottom.

Finishing

Refer to "Finishing" on page 14 to layer, baste, quilt and add the binding.

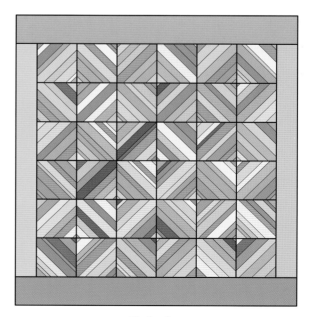

Quilt plan

LAND OF
NEW MEXICO
ENCHANTMENT

on the road again

INTERSTATE
US

VOLUNTEER
TENNESSEE
STATE

on the road again

Lost

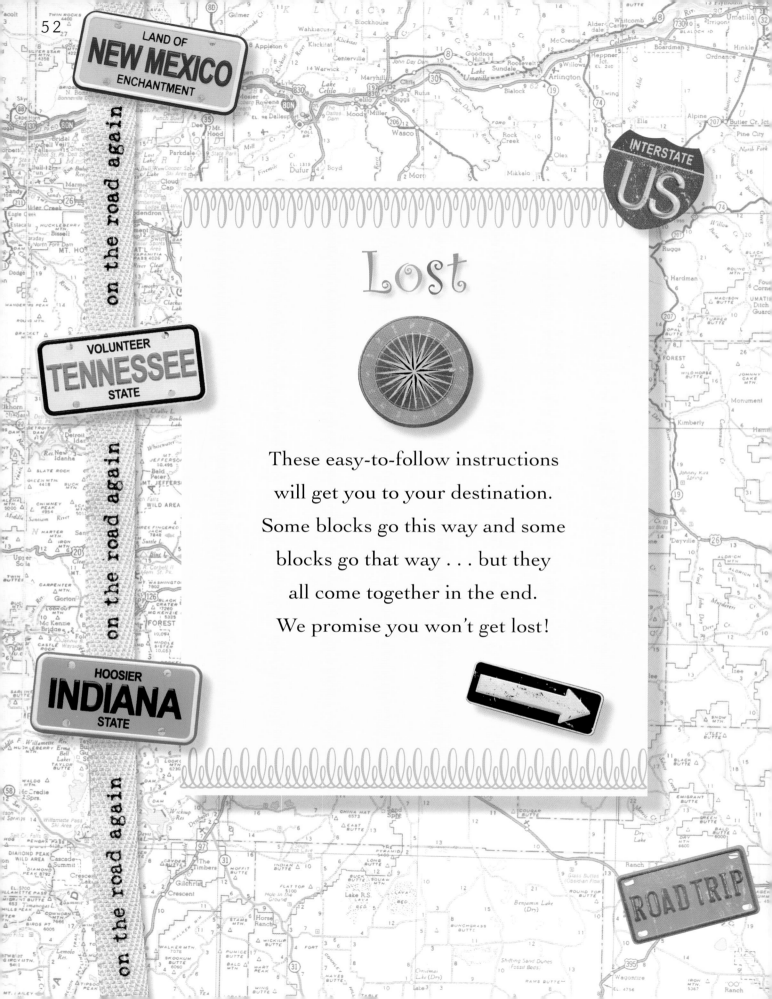

These easy-to-follow instructions
will get you to your destination.
Some blocks go this way and some
blocks go that way . . . but they
all come together in the end.
We promise you won't get lost!

HOOSIER
INDIANA
STATE

on the road again

ROAD TRIP

Designed and pieced by Mary Jacobson and Barbara Groves

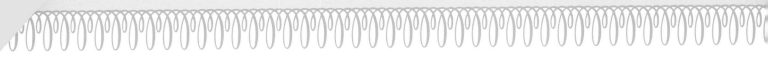

Finished quilt: 65" x 65" • Finished block: 7½" x 7½"

Materials

All yardages are based on 40"- wide fabric
2 yards of black dot for blocks
1 yard of green fabric for blocks and border
1 yard of turquoise fabric for blocks and border
1 yard of purple fabric for blocks and border
1 yard of pink fabric for blocks and border
¾ yard of orange fabric for blocks
¾ yard of blue fabric for blocks
¾ yard of blue fabric for binding
4¼ yards of fabric for backing
73" x 73" piece of batting

Cutting

FROM THE BLACK DOT, CUT:
24 strips, 2½" x 40"; crosscut into 384 squares,
    2½" x 2½"

**FROM *EACH* ORANGE, BLUE, GREEN, TUR-
QUOISE, PURPLE, AND PINK FABRIC, CUT:**
4 strips, 3" x 40"; crosscut into 32 rectangles,
    3" x 4½" (192 total)
5 strips, 2¼" x 40"; crosscut into 22 rectangles,
    2¼" x 8" (132 total; you will have 4 extra)

**FROM *EACH* GREEN, TURQUOISE, PURPLE, AND
PINK FABRIC, CUT:**
2 strips, 2¾" x 40" (8 total)

FROM BLUE FABRIC FOR BINDING, CUT:
7 strips, 2¼" x 40"

Making the Blocks

1. Draw a diagonal line on the wrong side of
   each 2½" black dot square.

2. With right sides together, place a 2½" black
   dot square on the corner of *each* 3" x 4½"

orange, blue, green, turquoise, purple, and
pink rectangle as shown.

3. Stitch on the marked line. Trim the seam
   allowances to ¼". Flip and press the seam
   allowances open.

4. With right sides together, place a second 2½"
   black dot square on the adjacent corner of
   each 3" x 4½" rectangle as shown.

5. Stitch on the marked line. Trim the seam
   allowances to ¼". Flip and press the seam
   allowances open. Make 32 of each color for a
   total of 192 flying-geese units.

Make 32 of each
color (192 total).

6. Separate the flying-geese units into two
   colorways: one with blue, turquoise, and
   purple and the other with green, orange,
   and pink.

7. To create the block centers, arrange and
   sew three flying-geese units from the blue,
   turquoise, and purple colorway as shown.
   Make 32. Shuffle the color placement for
   variety.

8. Sew a blue, turquoise, or purple 2¼" x 8"
   rectangle to each side
   of the block centers as
   shown. Make 32 of block
   A. You will have two extra
   rectangles. The blocks
   should now measure
   8" square.

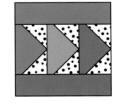

Block A.
Make 32.

9. Using the green, orange, and pink flying-geese units and rectangles, repeat steps 7–8 to make 32 of block B.

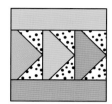

Block B.
Make 32.

Assembling the Quilt

1. Arrange and sew four of each block into a row as shown. Alternate the block color and direction. Make 8 rows.

Make 8.

2. Rotate every other row and sew them together as shown in the quilt plan at right. The quilt should now measure 60½" square.

Borders

1. Piece the two 2¾" x 40" purple strips end to end and piece the two 2¾" x 40" turquoise strips end to end. The purple strip will be attached to one side of the quilt and the turquoise strip will be attached to the opposite side.

2. Measure the quilt from top to bottom through the middle to determine the length of the side borders.

3. From *each* pieced length, cut the border to the measured length. Attach the purple border to one side of the quilt and the turquoise border to the opposite side.

4. Piece the two 2¾" x 40" pink border strips end to end and the two 2¾" x 40" green border strips end to end. The pink strip will be attached to the top of the quilt and the green will be attached to the bottom.

5. Measure the quilt from side to side through the middle including the side borders to determine the length of the top and bottom borders.

6. From *each* pieced length, cut the borders to the measured length. Attach the pink strip to the top and the green strip to the bottom of the quilt.

Finishing

Refer to "Finishing" on page 14 to layer, baste, quilt, and add the binding.

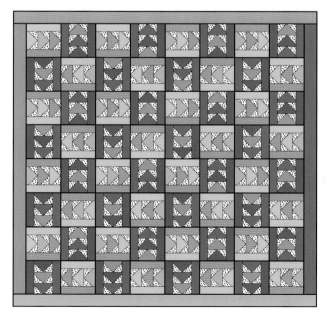

Quilt plan

I Know What You Did at Quilt Camp

We love going to quilt camps and retreats with our friends! Sometimes this is the only chance we get to see them and catch up on all the gossip! We like to keep our projects at camp cute and simple, leaving plenty of time for talking and eating.

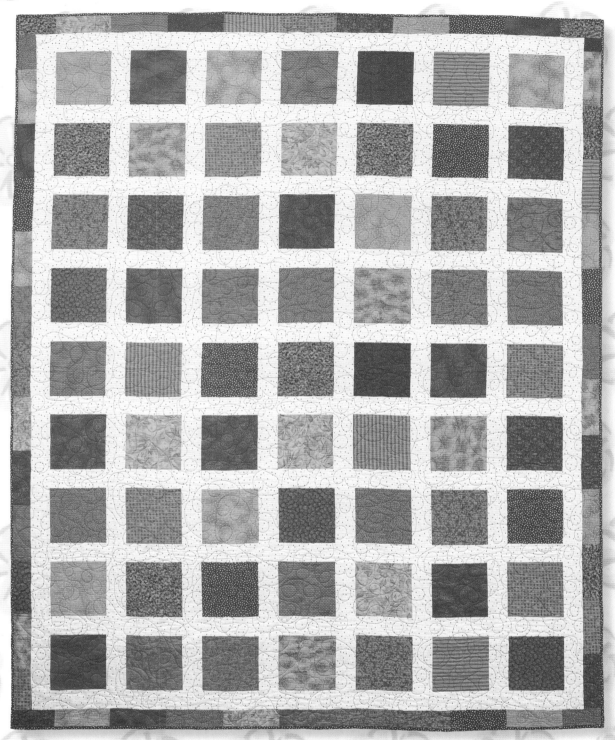

Designed and pieced by Barbara Groves and Mary Jacobson

Finished quilt: 74½" x 93" • Finished block: 7" x 7"

Materials

All yardages are based on 40"- wide fabric

24 fat quarters of pink prints for blocks and second
    border

3 yards of pink dot for sashing and first border

¾ yard of dark pink fabric for binding

8¾ yards of fabric for backing

83" x 102" piece of batting

Cutting

FROM EACH FAT QUARTER OF PINK PRINT, CUT:

3 squares, 7½" x 7½" (72 total)

2 rectangles, 3" x 7½" (48 total for second border)

FROM THE PINK DOT, CUT:

25 strips, 3" x 40"; from 11 of these strips cut 54
    rectangles, 3" x 7½"

8 strips, 3" x 40"

FROM THE DARK PINK FABRIC, CUT:

9 strips, 2¼" x 40"

Assembling the Quilt

1. Arrange and sew seven 7½" pink squares and
   six 3" x 7½" pink dot sashing rectangles into
   rows as shown. Make nine. You will have nine
   extra pink squares.

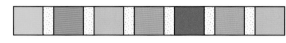

Make 9.

2. Piece the 14 pink dot 3" x 40" strips end to
   end. Press the seam allowances open.

3. From the pieced length cut eight strips,
   3" x 64½".

4. Sew together the block rows and sashing as
   shown in the quilt plan on page 59, beginning
   and ending with a block row. The quilt should
   now measure 64½" x 83½".

First Border

Piece the eight 3" x 40" pink dot strips end to end.
Refer to "Measuring and Adding Borders" on page
13 to cut and attach the first border. The quilt
should now measure 69½" x 88½".

Second Border

Piece the 48 pink 3" x 7½" rectangles end to end. Measure, cut, and attach the second border as you did the first.

Finishing

Refer to "Finishing" on page 14 to layer, baste, quilt, and add the binding.

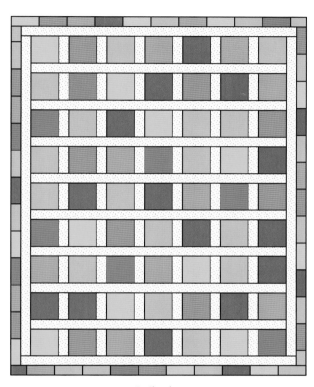

Quilt plan

Maui Waui

Let this tropical floral
be the inspiration to daydream
yourself to a faraway island.
Have fun beachcombing for your
favorite green and purple fabrics
to make this relaxing quilt.
It's sure to become a favorite!

Designed and pieced by Barbara Groves and Mary Jacobson

Finished quilt: 63" x 63" • Finished block: 10" x 10"

Materials

All yardages are based on 40"- wide fabric

2⅓ yards of large floral print for sashing and border

1½ yards of purple dot for blocks

⅓ yard *each* of 4 green fabrics for blocks

⅓ yard *each* of 4 purple fabrics for blocks

¾ yard of light purple fabric for binding

4¼ yards for backing

71" x 71" piece of batting

Cutting

FROM EACH OF THE GREEN AND PURPLE FABRICS, CUT:

2 strips, 2⅞" x 40"; crosscut into 16 squares,
    2⅞" x 2⅞" (128 total)

1 strip, 2½" x 40"; crosscut into 8 squares,
    2½" x 2½" (64 total; keep each print
    together and set aside)

FROM THE PURPLE DOT, CUT:

10 strips, 2⅞" x 40"; crosscut into 128 squares,
    2⅞" x 2⅞"

5 strips, 2½" x 40"; crosscut into 80 squares,
    2½" x 2½"

FROM THE LARGE FLORAL PRINT, CUT:

8 strips, 3½" x 40"; crosscut 4 of these strips into
    12 rectangles, 3½" x 10½"

6 strips, 7¼" x 40"

FROM THE LIGHT PURPLE FABRIC, CUT:

7 strips, 2¼" x 40"

Making the Blocks

1. Draw a diagonal line on the wrong side of each 2⅞" purple dot square.

2. With right sides together, layer a marked purple dot 2⅞" square and a green 2⅞" square. Stitch ¼" away from each side of the drawn line. Cut apart on the marked line and press the seam allowances open. The half-square triangles should measure 2½" square. Make 32 half-square triangles from each green print for a total of 128. Keep each print together.

Make 128.

3. Repeat step 2 with the remaining purple dot 2⅞" squares and the purple 2⅞" squares. Make 32 half-square triangles from each purple print for a total of 128. Keep each print together.

Make 128.

4. Keeping all half-square triangles and 2½" squares of the same color and print together, pair a green with a purple; arrange the squares into four combinations of one green print and one purple print. The combinations will remain together from now on.

5. From the first combination, arrange 12 green half-square triangles, four purple half-square

triangles, four purple 2½"
squares, and five purple dot
2½" squares into blocks.
Make two.

Make 2.

6. From the first combination,
arrange 12 purple half-square
triangles, four green half-
square triangles, four green
2½" squares, and five purple
dot 2½" squares into blocks.
Make two.

Make 2.

7. Repeat steps 5 and 6 for the remaining three
combinations for a total of 16 blocks.

Assembling the Quilt

1. Starting with a block with a green center and
ending with a block with a purple center,
arrange four blocks and three 3½" x 10½"
sashing rectangles into rows as shown.
Make two.

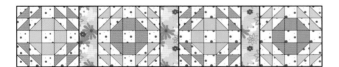

Make 2.

2. Starting with a block with a purple center
and ending with a block with a green center,
arrange four blocks and three 3½" x 10½"
sashing rectangles into rows as shown.
Make two.

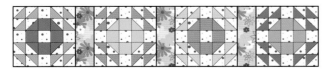

Make 2.

Sashing

1. Piece four 3½" x 40" sashing strips end to
end. Press the seam allowances open. Cut
the pieced length into three 49½" lengths.

2. Arrange and sew the block rows with the
sashing as shown in the quilt plan below.

Border

Piece the six 7¼" x 40" large floral strips together
end to end. Press the seam allowances open.
Refer to "Measuring and Adding Borders" on page
13 to cut and attach the border.

Finishing

Refer to "Finishing" on page 14 to layer, baste,
quilt, trim, and add the binding.

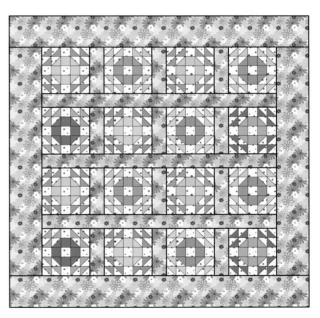

Quilt plan

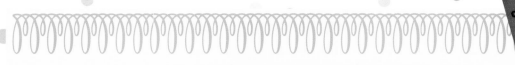

About the Authors

YES, THEY REALLY ARE sisters! Barbara Groves and
Mary Jacobson of Me and My Sister Designs have shared
a love of fabric, sewing, and quilting for almost as long as
they have been sisters. They are involved in almost every
aspect of quiltmaking.

Their belief in fast, fun, and easy designs can be seen
in the quilts created for their pattern company, in their
many books, and in their fabric designs for Moda.

Barb and Mary both live in Phoenix, Arizona, with
their families. They see each other almost every day.

See what's up next for these two by visiting their
Web site: meandmysisterdesigns.com.